THE TABLETOP LEARNING SERIES

NATURE CRAFTS

Simple Pleasures with Natural Treasures
by Imogene Forte

Incentive Publications, Inc.
Nashville, Tennessee

Illustrated by Susan Eaddy
Cover designed by Mary Hamilton and illustrated by Becky Cutler
Edited by Susan Oglander

Library of Congress Catalog Number 84-62931
ISBN 0-86530-098-4

Copyright © 1985 by Incentive Publications, Inc., Nashville, Tennessee. All rights reserved. No part of this publication may be reproduced, stored in a retrieval system, or transmitted in any way or by any means (electronic, mechanical, photocopying, recording, or otherwise) without prior written permission from Incentive Publications, Inc.

THE TABLETOP LEARNING SERIES™ is a trademark of Incentive Publications, Inc., Nashville, TN 37215

THIS
NATURE CRAFTS BOOK
BELONGS TO

_____

CONTENTS

A NOTE TO KIDS

This book is about appreciating and making things with nature's treasures. Many of the materials you will need are right under your nose on "your own turf." Others may be easily collected on trips to the beach, fields and woods. All are yours for the taking because the projects call for only things that may be collected without disturbing the natural environment. Seashells, driftwood, beach grasses, rocks, small plants from the waterways; sand, leaves, fruits and vegetables, flowers, feathers and weeds from yards, sidewalks or parks; cones, reeds, branches, twigs, bark, corn shucks and vines from the fields and woodlands will all be easily spotted once you have trained yourself to be on the lookout for them.

Some of the projects include easy, step-by-step instructions for making useful or decorative items to give for gifts or to keep and enjoy. Others however, are just to experiment with. Most cost little or nothing but your time. Actually, if you have scissors, glue, crayons, pencils, paints, and some of nature's treasures, you are all set.

The purpose of this little book is to help you become aware of, appreciate and make creative use of nature's bounty.

Imogene Forte

YOUR OWN TURF

YOUR STOMPING GROUND

Do you look for interesting rocks and unusual pebbles on your way to school? Would you know where to find sand or gravel if you needed it? Have you noticed tiny plants creeping up between the cracks in the sidewalk? Do you observe the changes in the trees in your neighborhood from the time the buds appear in the spring until the leaves change color and drop in the fall? Do you examine and sometimes carry home cones and seedpods that you find along the roadside or in the park? Do you watch the flowers and weeds wake up from their long winter sleep to bud and blossom? Have you planted seeds from fruits and vegetables in your own kitchen for a windowsill or outdoor garden? Do you know which berries and seeds the birds in your neighborhood feed on?

If you answered yes to two, three or more of these questions, you probably are well on your way to observing and appreciating the natural treasures provided by "your own turf."

The activities in this section will show you how to use the objects that you find on the ground, under trees, near fences, around shrubs and bushes, along the sidewalk and even in mud puddles to make all sorts of wonderful things. You will need to study your environment carefully and collect only things that will not disturb the delicate balance of nature. When in doubt, ask someone in charge.

So you see, you don't have to go to the seashore, the desert or the mountaintops to collect materials to use in nature craft projects — you have everything you need right under your own nose! The important thing is to begin to use your imagination and look around for things to use in new and creative ways. You will be surprised at how many things you see that you never noticed before.

RUB-A-DUB-DUB — LEAVES, BARK AND STONES TO RUB

Making rubbings of natural materials helps you to see them in a whole new light. Details that you might not notice begin to appear, and before you know it, you have a most interesting design.

WHAT TO USE:
- white paper
- pencil, charcoal or crayon
- bark, shells, flat stones, leaves

WHAT TO DO:
1.   Place the paper on a flat surface over any natural material you would like to make a rubbing of. When rubbing leaves, be sure to turn the bottom side of the leaf up so that the veins will show up.

2. Rub the broad side of your pencil point, crayon or charcoal back and forth over the paper. Continue until the whole surface of the object has been rubbed.

3. The lines, bumps, holes, grooves and veins will show up in an entirely different way.

4. Some of your rubbings will probably be so special you will want to frame them. If so, you can use an inexpensive frame (or an old one you already have) or make one from heavy construction paper and cover the rubbing with clear plastic wrap.

MAKING NATURAL FACES

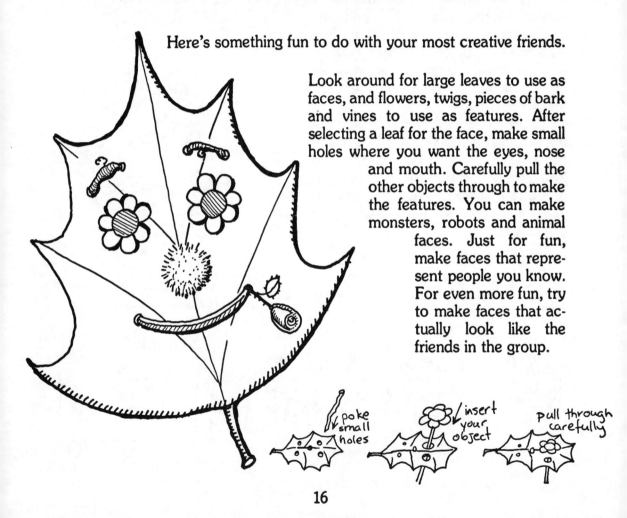

Here's something fun to do with your most creative friends.

Look around for large leaves to use as faces, and flowers, twigs, pieces of bark and vines to use as features. After selecting a leaf for the face, make small holes where you want the eyes, nose and mouth. Carefully pull the other objects through to make the features. You can make monsters, robots and animal faces. Just for fun, make faces that represent people you know. For even more fun, try to make faces that actually look like the friends in the group.

poke small holes

insert your object

pull through carefully

16

MOSAIC MASTERPIECE

Collect smooth pebbles, small stones, seeds, pieces of twigs and other small, hard materials to use for mosaic designs.

Use Styrofoam meat trays, covers from nut or coffee cans or aluminum pie pans for a base. Beginning in the center, build a design with the objects. Arrange the design carefully to bring out and show off the color, shape and texture of the materials before you begin to glue them in place.

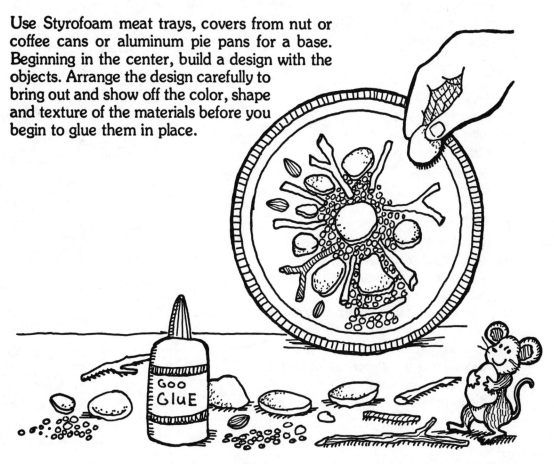

SEAL-A-DESIGN

Save the loveliest ferns, graceful vines and brilliantly-colored leaves from an autumn outing to brighten up a gloomy winter day.

WHAT TO USE:
- leaves, ferns, short pieces of vine with interesting leaves
- construction paper
- waxed paper
- iron

WHAT TO DO:
1. Place a sheet of waxed paper on top of a sheet of construction paper.
2. Arrange the leaves, ferns or vines on the waxed paper.
3. Place a second sheet of waxed paper on top and cover with another sheet of construction paper.
4. Slowly move a warm iron over the top of the construction paper to seal the design inside.

waxed paper

construction paper

waxed paper

leaves

construction paper

iron to seal in design, remove construction paper

ARTICHOKE CANDLEHOLDERS

Select two dried artichokes that are just about the same size. Remove the stems and peel off enough of the leaves to make them sit squarely. Pull out enough of the center section to make a space just right to hold an upright candle. Stick a candle in the space and you will have a "natural" light for a special occasion.

If you have artichokes aplenty, you might arrange several in a basket or wooden bowl. Place the basket between the two candleholders — this centerpiece would look lovely on a mantel or dining table.

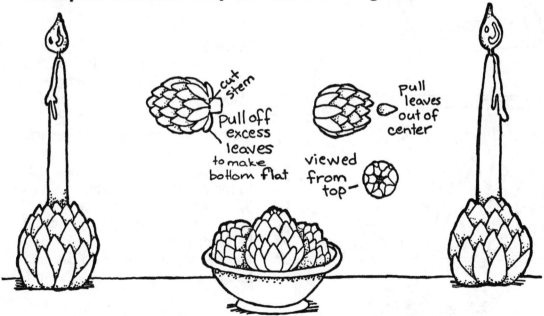

BOX TOP DESIGN

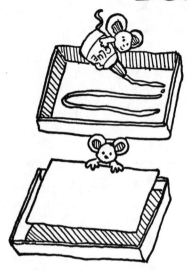

WHAT TO USE:

- a sturdy box top (from stationery or a shoe box)
- construction paper
- glue
- scissors
- natural materials such as small stones, dried leaves, twigs, pebbles, vines, etc.

WHAT TO DO:

1. Cover the back of the box top with construction paper and glue in place. Choose a color of paper for the inside that you would like for the background of your scene and glue it in place.
2. Arrange the natural materials to form a scene you like.
3. Carefully lift each object, put a little glue on it and gently press it back into place.
4. Allow your design to dry and hang it on the wall or give it as a gift.

PRINTER'S PRESS

Once you begin using natural materials to print with, you will see all sorts of possibilities for interesting and unusual designs.

All you need is paper, paint and the object you wish to print. Simply brush paint on one side of the object, or if it is easier, dip the object in the paint. Then, press the object down firmly on your paper. By repeatedly "printing" your object on paper, you can create many interesting designs.

After it dries, your printed paper can be used as a wall hanging, as gift wrap, a greeting card or to cover wastebaskets and trinket boxes. Try some of these objects to help you get started.

PRESSED POSIES

The best time to pick the flowers you want to press is early in the morning while they are nice and fresh. If some of them still have traces of dew, let them dry a bit first.

Press the flowers between tissue paper or paper towels. Leave plenty of space in between the blossoms. Place the flowers between thick piles of newspaper and then under a large stack of books. After about two weeks, your flowers will be ready to use.

CUT AND DRIED

To preserve the beauty of flowers, you can follow these instructions for a bouquet that will last much more than a few days.

WHAT TO USE:
- cornmeal
- borax
- shoe box (or something similar)
- paintbrush
- flowers, leaves, etc.

WHAT TO DO:
1. Mix equal parts of cornmeal and borax.
2. Pour a one-inch layer of the mixture into the box.
3. Carefully lay the flowers out on the mixture.
4. Sprinkle more of the mixture on top of the flowers.
5. Put the top on the box and set aside in a dry place for two to three weeks.
6. Gently remove the flowers from the box and brush off the mixture with a dry paintbrush.

THINGS TO DO WITH PRESSED OR DRIED FLOWERS

Pressed Flowers
- glue some on a wide piece of ribbon and tie it on as a headband
- decorate a very special Valentine
- dress up a bookmark
- glue on plain paper to make stationery and give it as a gift

Dried Flowers

- use as a special touch when wrapping a gift
- glue some extra pretty dried flowers onto a hair comb and wear it for a fancy occasion
- combine with dried orange and grapefruit peel, cinnamon sticks, cloves and allspice to make a fragrant potpourri

FANCY FEATHERS

Collect bird, chicken, turkey, duck or goose
feathers to use to make very special greeting
cards.

Use different kinds of paper and felt
tip pens to make extra creative
cards. Plan your designs so that
adding a feather for interest will
give a most unusual flair.

NUTS TO YOU

Try some of these nutty designs ...

Mighty Mouse

felt circles

draw face with markers

straw whiskers

Pecan Patsy

cloth tied around nut

button ear-rings sewn to cloth

use paint or markers for face

Peanut Pals

pipe cleaner

seed eyes

Pipe cleaner pushed through peanut for tail, ears + legs use straw for whiskers

Theodore Turtle

clay

feet of clay

APPLE HEAD ANGELS

Peel the apple 1st —

make indentions
with your fingers

Peel a small apple. Press eyes, nose and a mouth into the apple with your finger tips. Put the apple away in a cool, dry place for about two weeks. Check periodically to see when it is shriveled and brown. Then it will be ready to use. Take the apple out and poke a stick into the bottom of it. Use white tissue paper and lace paper doilies to "dress" your angel. If you want to get real fancy, you could add sequins, beads, ribbons and yarn hair.

poke sharp
stick through
center of
doily and
then into
bottom of
apple

two
weeks
later

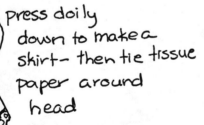

Press doily
down to make a
skirt — then tie tissue
paper around
head

cut pieces from
a doily for wings
and halo

28

Your angel can be used to decorate the top of your Christmas tree or as a centerpiece, puppet or gift for a special friend.

glue on wings and halo

SPEEDY GOURDZALES

WHAT TO USE:
- gourd
- soapy water
- enamel or poster paints and paintbrush

WHAT TO DO:
1. Select a firm gourd with a fairly long neck.
2. Wash the gourd in soapy water and dry thoroughly.
3. Paint your gourd to resemble a Spanish bandito.

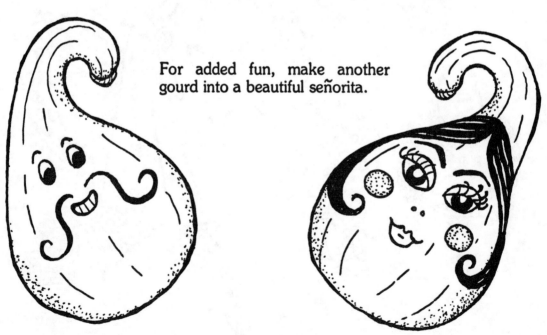

For added fun, make another gourd into a beautiful señorita.

AN AGING MARTIAN

WHAT TO USE:
- avocado
- frill picks
- glue
- pipe cleaners
- buttons
- straight pins

WHAT TO DO:
1. Stand the avocado on a table covered with newspaper.
2. Insert the frill picks at the top for antennae.
3. Stick the pins in the buttons and push on for eyes.
4. Form a nose and mouth with pipe cleaners and glue on.
5. Sit your Martian in a windowsill on a plate.
6. Watch your Martian for a few days and note the changes. In a short time, your Martian will look like he's growing old.

31

BE KIND TO MOTHER NATURE

As you explore your favorite "natural" places, you may find some litter left by those who don't appreciate nature the way you do. Think of the pretty pictures you can create by cleaning up the mess.

THINGS TO DO WITH LITTER

cut plastic for fish

make a seascape in a bottle

Cover cans with paper and make a mobile

RECYCLING CENTER

QUICKIES
Just For Fun With Treasures From Your Own Turf

- Find a blade of grass to use as a whistle.
- Have fun with posy puppets (hollyhock blossoms are great for this).
- Make chains of clover or dandelion jewelry.
- Make mud pies.
- Make a circus parade, a zoo or just a funny animal or two from the vegetables in your kitchen, a little paper, glue and a pencil.
- Cut off the top of a carrot, pineapple or turnip and stick it in a saucer of water on your windowsill. Then watch to see how long it takes to begin to "grow."
- Carefully open a walnut. Eat the meat and use the shell to hold a note or tiny gift. Glue the walnut shell back together and give it to someone who knows how to appreciate a surprise.

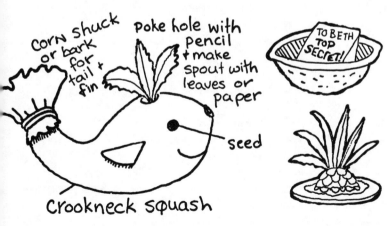

Corn shuck or bark for tail + fin

Poke hole with pencil + make spout with leaves or paper

seed

Crookneck squash

TO BETH TOP SECRET!

Glue paper wings on a carrot + make a butterfly

THROUGH WOODS AND FIELDS

HEAD FOR THE WOODS

When planning a day in the woods or countryside, prepare ahead to preserve some of the day's special beauty. As you strap on your backpack, be sure to include several plastic or paper bags to carry home your very best "finds." In addition to the sights, sounds and smells of a walk through the woods or a bike ride down a country road, keep your eyes open for the small treasures you can find just about everywhere. Be careful not to destroy things which would upset the natural environment, but do take time to gather such things as fallen apples, nuts, pine cones, sticks, stones, moss, flowers, weeds, berries, seedpods and beautifully colored feathers. Preserving and displaying the contents of the bags you fill from these special areas will bring back memories and provide hours of creative projects.

TIE UP A BUNDLE OF WARM WISHES

As you go exploring in the woods, you will see many twigs and branches that have fallen or been blown from trees to lie unnoticed on the ground. Free for the taking, they make great fire starters for people who have wood stoves or fireplaces.

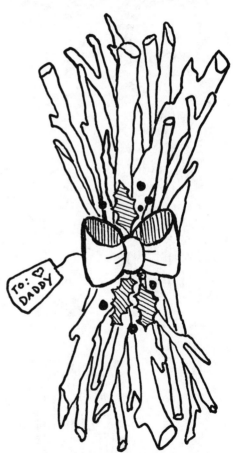

Gather them by the bagful (large shopping bags are good to carry them in) and take them home to arrange in bundles. Tie each bundle securely with heavy string or cord, add a fancy bow, some pine cones, a sprig of greenery and some red berries (if you were lucky enough to find some) and you will have a lovely and useful gift that is sure to carry your "warm wishes."

PINE NEEDLE CREATIONS

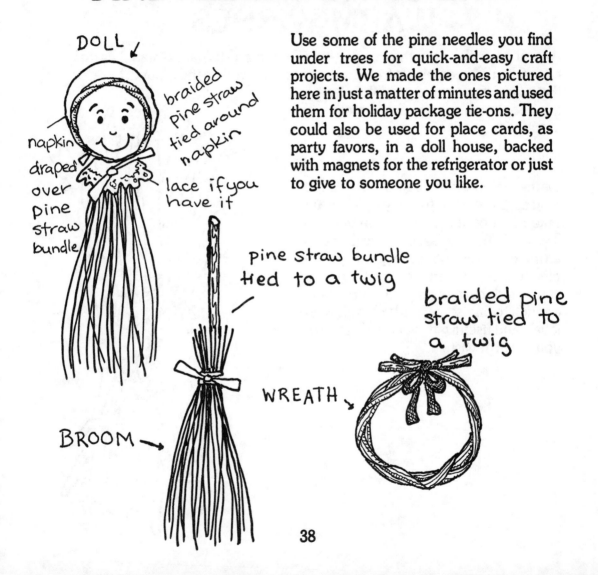

DOLL

braided pine straw tied around napkin

napkin draped over pine straw bundle

lace if you have it

Use some of the pine needles you find under trees for quick-and-easy craft projects. We made the ones pictured here in just a matter of minutes and used them for holiday package tie-ons. They could also be used for place cards, as party favors, in a doll house, backed with magnets for the refrigerator or just to give to someone you like.

pine straw bundle tied to a twig

braided pine straw tied to a twig

BROOM →

WREATH →

38

CAN YOU IMAGINE A SCULPTURE SO FINE?

While you are collecting twigs and sticks, be on the lookout for interesting-shaped ones to use for a sculpture. Turn the twigs around and around, stand them up straight, lay them out flat, place two back to back — the secret here is to look for ordinary things in an extra-ordinary way. As you keep arranging and rearranging the twigs and sticks, an interesting free-form design will begin to appear right before your eyes. Glue the design into place if you need to. Sometimes, the twigs just hold their own without any help. Add seeds, pebbles or pieces of bark if you like.

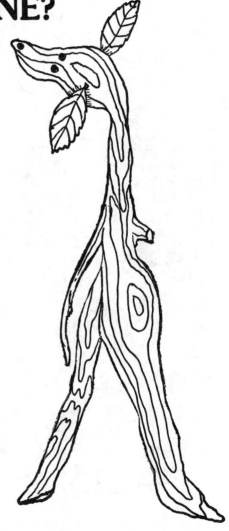

IN SEARCH OF MOSS

WHAT TO USE:
- moss (found in trees and on vines and bushes)
- dried flowers
- sewing thread

WHAT TO DO:
1. Put on your walking shoes and get ready to wander through the woods in search of moss. The type of moss you will find will vary depending on where you live. Carry along a basket to gather the moss in. You may need to find a stick to gently knock the moss out of the trees if it's too high to reach.

40

2. Then, once you get back to your work space, you simply shape the moss into a wreath.

3. Weave a piece of thread through the moss to hold it together and knot it at the back.

4. Tie on dried flowers to decorate your wreath.

You can follow the same directions to make a bird's nest, too. They make great Christmas tree decorations or Easter baskets.

use pebbles for eggs

DESIGN A HAT AND WEAR IT

A fun thing to do with a friend or two on a hot summer day is to use natural materials to design a hat to make and wear.

Your hat may turn out to be much more charming and creative than you might think. First, you will need to look around for the materials to use. Leaves may be hooked together by their own stems; seedpods, cones, acorn caps, burs and teasels may be glued to vines and shaped into a coronet; twigs can be shaped and glued together to make a headband; or a beret or skullcap can be woven from grasses.

Look for seedpods, a feather, a cluster of shells, flowers or anything else you can find to give your hat that finishing touch.

NUT AND CONE TREE

WHAT TO USE:
- lots of small natural objects (nuts, seedpods, pine cones, pine needles)
- lightweight cardboard
- stapler or tape
- heavy-duty glue
- clear spray shellac
- old saucer or aluminum pie pan

WHAT TO DO:
1. Collect interesting nuts, seedpods and cones.
2. Make a cone from lightweight cardboard and glue it together.
3. Glue seeds, nuts, etc., on the cone so that the cardboard is no longer visible.
4. Let it dry for approximately one hour.
5. Then, glue the bottom of the cardboard cone to the saucer.
6. After the glue has dried, spray shellac on the saucer and cone.

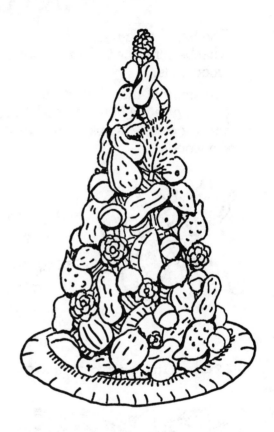

HAPPY HOLIDAYS NATURALLY

The best holiday gifts and decorations are those you make yourself. And, what better place is there to look for materials to use than in open fields and woodlands?

Try some of these for starters, and then let your imagination take over. (These give the house a good "woodsy" smell and are sure to be welcome gifts for elderly people or friends who are not able to enjoy a winter walk in the woods.)

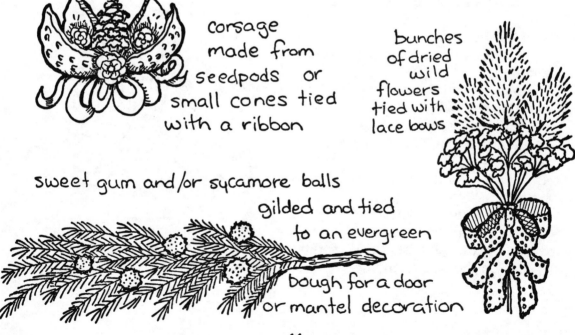

corsage made from seedpods or small cones tied with a ribbon

bunches of dried wild flowers tied with lace bows

sweet gum and/or sycamore balls gilded and tied to an evergreen bough for a door or mantel decoration

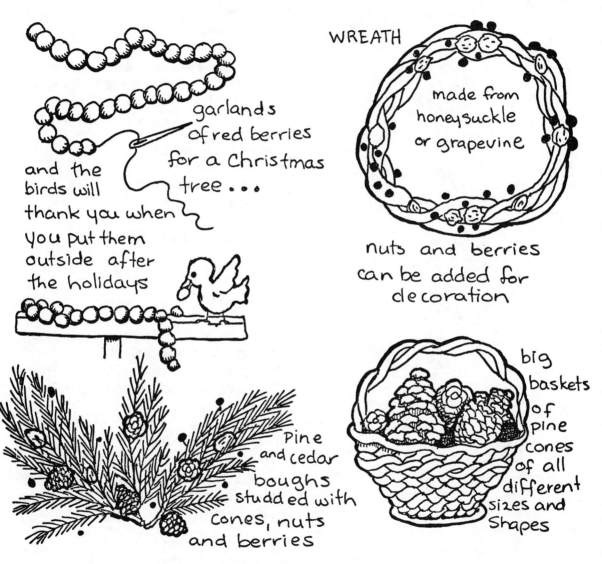

garlands of red berries for a Christmas tree . . .

and the birds will thank you when you put them outside after the holidays

WREATH

made from honeysuckle or grapevine

nuts and berries can be added for decoration

Pine and cedar boughs studded with cones, nuts and berries

big baskets of pine cones of all different sizes and shapes

45

AW SHUCKS!

You can use these napkin rings for any special dinner or lunch and they will surely brighten the meal.

WHAT TO USE:
- dried corn husks
- warm water
- glue
- scissors
- ribbon or seedpods

WHAT TO DO:
1. Use scissors to cut the corn husks into strips wide enough to braid. (You can tear them if you want.)
2. Soak the husk strips in warm water.
3. Braid three strips into a ring large enough to hold a napkin.
4. Cut the ends off evenly and glue them together at the top. You may need to let them dry a bit before gluing.
5. When thoroughly dry, add a piece of ribbon or a seedpod to give them that extra touch.

CONE CREATURES

OWL

Collect cones and seedpods of different sizes and shapes. Fool around with the materials to see what strange or unusual creatures their shapes suggest to you. Then, look for ...

- a smooth, flat stone to use for a base
- seeds, twigs or pieces of bark to make facial features, ears, a tail, etc.

Shape your creature and glue it together. Then glue it onto the base. Add the features and set your creature on a shelf where you can enjoy it.

Turkey

Turtle

47

QUICKIES
Just For Fun With Treasures From The Woods And Fields

Play "he loves me, he loves me not" by pulling the petals from a daisy as you count off.

Blow milkweed seed parachutes into the air and see how far you can make them fly.

Fill a pine cone with cookie crumbs, peanut butter or leftovers from a picnic. Tie a string around it and hang it in a tree for the hungry birds.

Make five-pointed stars from leaves and small seedpods or cones. Just shape your star and push the stem of the seedpod through the center (where the ends of the leaves overlap) to hold the star together.

Collect a big bunch of dried weeds with interesting foliage to take home to use as a bouquet.

Make insects from maple seeds, fairy drinking cups from acorn caps and mice from teasels.

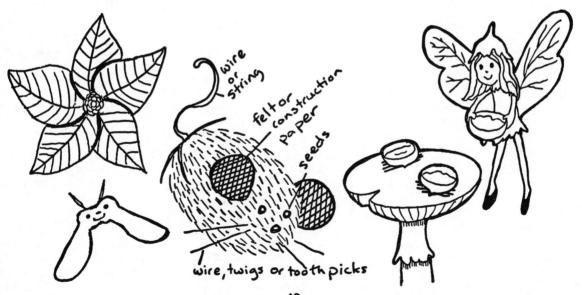

wire or string

felt or construction paper

seeds

wire, twigs or toothpicks

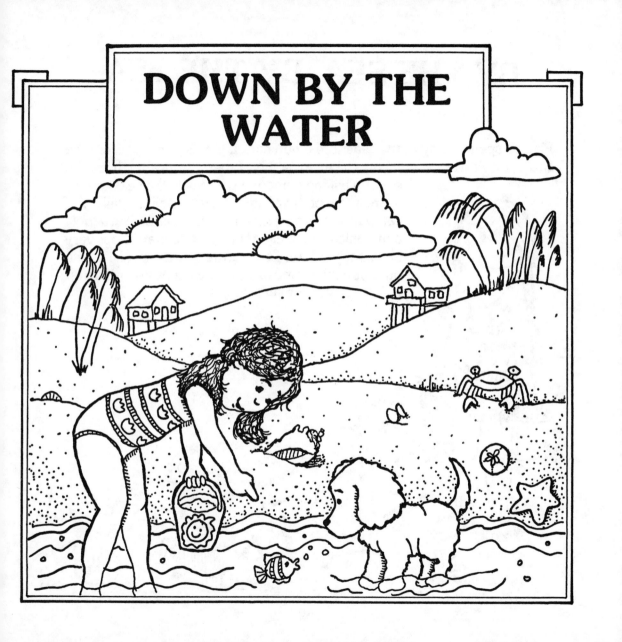

DOWN BY THE WATER

BY THE SEA, BY THE SEA

Plan to spend a day at the seashore if you can. If you live too far from the shore, don't worry. You can still make some of these "treasures from the sea" by asking someone who visits the seashore to share some of their finds with you. If all else fails, you can buy sand from plant nurseries or building supply companies and shells at import and craft shops very inexpensively. While they are not as special as the ones you might find on your own, they will bring a bit of the seashore magic to you.

Build A Fine Castle

Use all the architectural skills you have to build a sand castle fit for a king and queen. Take enough time to add towers, turrets, windows, doors and tunnels — maybe even a moat to keep the enemy out. Building sand castles lets you use your imagination to the fullest, and can be very exciting. But remember, time and tide wait for no man. Today your castle is a work of art, tomorrow there may be no trace of your masterpiece.

Try Your Hand At Sculpture, Too

While you have all your equipment together and the sand is just right, think of an animal, famous person, creature from another planet or even a car of the future that you would like to create.

Brush And Comb The Sand Into Shape

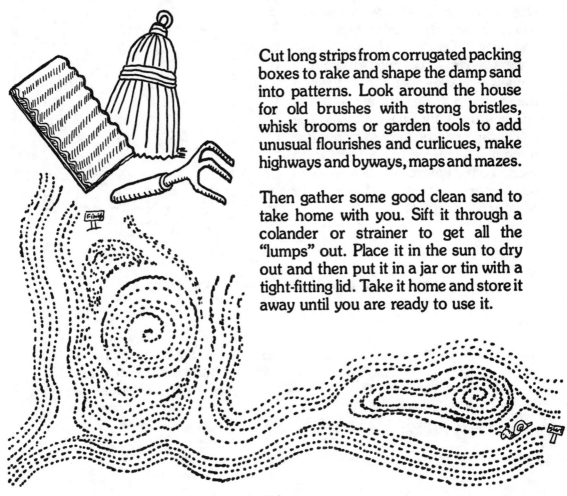

Cut long strips from corrugated packing boxes to rake and shape the damp sand into patterns. Look around the house for old brushes with strong bristles, whisk brooms or garden tools to add unusual flourishes and curlicues, make highways and byways, maps and mazes.

Then gather some good clean sand to take home with you. Sift it through a colander or strainer to get all the "lumps" out. Place it in the sun to dry out and then put it in a jar or tin with a tight-fitting lid. Take it home and store it away until you are ready to use it.

Sand Painting

The next time you are bored and want to remember your pleasant day at the seashore, gather your materials and make a sand painting.

draw a simple picture and brush glue inside the outlines

mix small amounts of sand with food coloring - pour the colored sand on your drawing

layer colored sand in a pretty jar -

Sand Scene

Another good way to use your sand is to make a scene in a jar.

or cover the bottom of a tank for a colorful terrarium

SEASHELLS BY THE SEASHORE

Of all nature's treasures, seashells are among the most interesting, and they certainly are fascinating to collect and use in arts and crafts projects.

The best time for serious shell collecting is after a storm, during low tide. But with a little patience, any early morning walk at the water's edge should yield enough shells to make the search worthwhile. Wash your shells and carry

them home in your pail. When you get home, clean them by soaking them in a solution of water and a little laundry bleach. If you find shells which have an unpleasant odor, soak them in alcohol. You need to check carefully when cleaning your shells however, because oversoaking can result in a loss of some of the shell's natural color. Put the washed shells on a picnic table (or other smooth surface) to dry in the sunshine.

An empty egg carton makes a great storage chest for small shells. Larger shells can be kept in baskets, plastic pails or even cardboard boxes. They can be organized by color, shape and size for later use in craft projects, or to display as a collection.

LOOK FOR THE RIGHT SHELLS

Look for a shell just the right size, shape and color to use to hold ...

potpourri

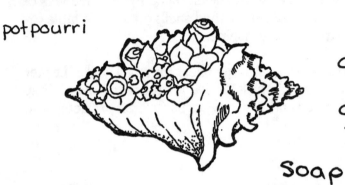

grasses
and
dried
flowers

a snack

try a tiny tossed salad

or pudding

Soap

you can decorate your soap
dish with smaller shells

Use your prettiest shells to decorate ...

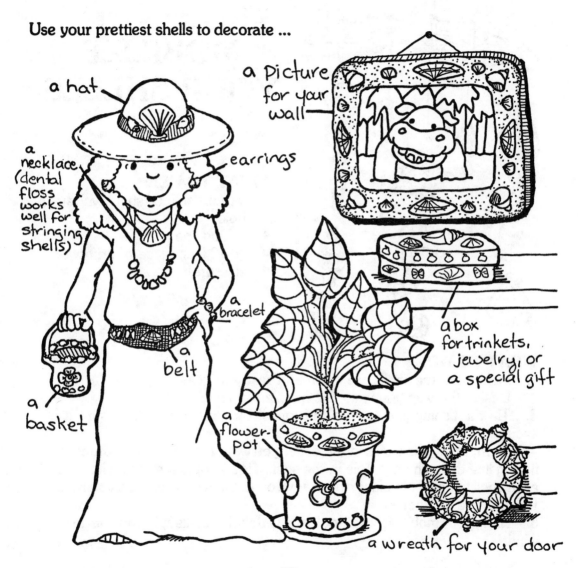

a hat

a picture for your wall

a necklace (dental floss works well for stringing shells)

earrings

a bracelet

a belt

a basket

a box for trinkets, jewelry, or a special gift

a flower-pot

a wreath for your door

59

MOBILIZE YOUR SHELLS

WHAT TO USE:
- various shaped shells with small holes
- fishing line
- 10-12 inch piece of driftwood
- scissors

WHAT TO DO:
1. Make sure the shells are clean and ready to use.
2. Design the way you want the mobile to look.
3. Tie the fishing line around the top of the driftwood. Make sure it is secure.
4. Then, string the shells in the order you want them to hang, putting the fishing line through each hole in the shell. Tie a knot in the fishing line after each shell to keep it in place, then move on to the next shell until you reach the end. Tie another knot.
5. Hang your mobile from a hook and watch the shells spin and twirl in the wind.

NATURE CREATURES ON THE MOVE

WHAT TO USE:
- posterboard
- felt tip pens or crayons
- snail, periwinkle or other small shells, pebbles, sticks, twigs, etc.
- glue

WHAT TO DO:
1. Look for snail shells, periwinkle shells or interesting-shaped small stones to turn into "creatures." Make one "creature" for each player.
2. Glue on small twigs, blades of grass or other finds for antennae.
3. Glue pebbles, sticks, twigs and other materials from the water's edge to form a scene on the posterboard.
4. Now, make up a game, complete with rules, to play on the game board with the nature "creatures."

CAPTURE THE BEACH IN A JAR

When it is snowing outside and visions of summer vacation are dancing in your head, chase the wintertime blues away with your own beach in a jar.

WHAT TO USE:
- a glass jar with a screw-on lid or clamp top
- clean sand
- shells, pebbles, pieces of coral
- laundry bleach

WHAT TO DO:
1. Place the sand in the bottom of the jar and shake it around to form drifts.
2. Arrange the shells, pieces of coral and pebbles in the sand. Try to arrange them so that the different levels look like real drifts at the beach. Stand some of the taller things up and lean others against them, pushing the sand around with your fingers. Use the most interesting shells you have to give interest to the scene. A sea horse, small sand dollar or zebra shell would be extra special. Smooth bits of bottle glass will add color, too.

3. Carefully fill the jar with water.
4. Add three tablespoons of laundry bleach to keep the water clear.
5. Replace the lid and glue on a few shells to finish your arrangement in style.

When you place your "beach in a jar" on a table to be enjoyed by the family, they may not be able to hear the sound of ocean waves, but they are sure to get your message.

If your vacation is going to be near a creek or a river rather than the ocean, follow the same procedure to make an underwater scene with gravel, pebbles, small stones, snail shells and other treasures from the creek bank.

CREEK TREK

Walk along the edge of your favorite creek to look for tiny plants that can be safely moved and replanted.

You will need ...
- a big fork, spoon and spatula
- a pail or pan to carry the plants home in
- jars or plastic bags for the pebbles, gravel and soil

When you find a plant that you want, loosen the soil around it with the fork and spoon. Use the spatula to carefully lift the plant into your pail, making sure some of the soil is still covering the roots. Look for tiny ferns, blooming plants and plants with interesting shaped leaves or buds. Limit your collection to small plants with good roots. Collect some pebbles, gravel and soil from the creek to use when transporting the plants.

GROW A GARDEN IN GLASS

Select a large bottle, an interesting jar or even a deep glass bowl to hold your garden from the creek's edge. Begin by putting some gravel or pebbles in the bottom of the container. Then, cover the pebbles with approximately two inches of soil. Add a few small pieces of charcoal to keep the terrarium sweet-smelling. You can mold the soil with your hands to make small mounds so your garden won't look so flat. Carefully place the plants in the soil, making an interesting arrangement as you go. Additional pebbles or pieces of wood can be used for decoration. If you have access to some pretty green moss, you can cover some of the soil with that. Sprinkle your terrarium with water until the soil is moist. Put your garden in a spot with some nice, indirect light.

TURN YOUR TERRARIUM INTO A VIVARIUM

You probably knew that a garden planted in a glass container is called a terrarium. But, did you know that when the same type of garden is planted to provide a home for small animals, it is called a vivarium? You can find small animals to add to your terrarium along the same creek bed where you find the plants.

For a vivarium you will probably want to use a larger container so that the animals will have room to move around freely. You will also want to cut a piece of screen wire to cover the top of the container and add a small bowl of water for the animals. The kind of animals you find will depend on where you live and the time of year you are hunting. Tiny turtles, snails and insects are good choices. Whatever animals you choose to inhabit your vivarium, don't

forget to change their water and to provide fresh food everyday. Remember too, that it is always wise to bring animals of any kind into the house for a visit rather than for a permanent stay. Just like you, they may enjoy a vacation, but they are healthier and happier in their own home.

THE ROCKY SIDE

While you are walking along the creek bank, you may want to look for interesting rocks to use in craft projects or just to add to a collection. The difference in just picking up stones and in being a real rockhound is focusing on quality rather than quantity. It is not how many, but what kind of rocks you collect that counts. Get a good book on rocks to use as a reference and begin to look for specific types.

When your collection begins to grow to the point where it includes several shapes, sizes and kinds of rocks, you may want to use some of them for one or more of the following projects.

Make animals by gluing several different sizes of rocks together and painting on facial features.

Paint a pretty design on an especially smooth one to make a paperweight.

Spread glue around the sides of a small frozen juice can and add the rocks to make a pencil holder. Work out the design on a piece of paper first in order to get a more interesting finished product.

FAKE A FOSSIL

A fossil is created when a plant or animal gets trapped during the rock making process. Even though this process usually takes years and years, you can experiment to find out how it happens.

play dough

You will need some damp clay or play dough, a small sturdy box or an aluminum foil tart pan, some plaster of Paris and the item you wish to "fossil ize." Some good items to use are seed-pods, shells, nuts, pieces of bark, feathers or bones. Here's what you do ...

1. Spread the damp clay or play dough in the bottom of the box or pan.
2. Press the item into the clay or play dough with your hand. Be sure it is pressed all the way in.
3. Mix the plaster of Paris with water to form a paste. (If you don't have plaster of Paris, you can use the kind of plaster used to patch plaster walls.)
4. Pour the plaster of Paris into the mold to completely cover the item.
5. Leave the plaster to dry overnight. Then, peel away the box or pan to reveal your own fossil creation.

Even though your fossil is cast in plaster rather than stone, the experiment will give you a better understanding of how real fossils are made and you will have a neat nature craft product for your collection.

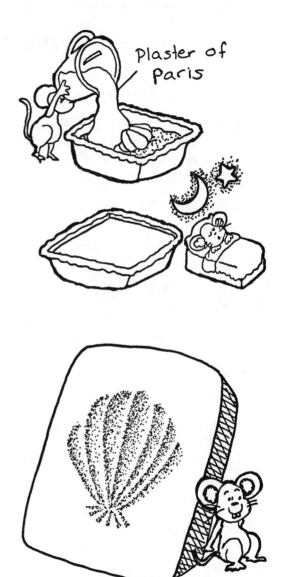

Plaster of Paris

69

DRIFTWOOD

Look for beautiful or odd-shaped pieces of driftwood. Use your imagination when deciding which pieces to take home with you.

Small pieces of driftwood may be painted to make wall plaques.

Even smaller pieces may be attractively arranged and glued on to make a jewelry box or paper clip container.

Other pieces may be used as the base for a mobile, as decorations for a flower or rock garden or for a door or gate decoration.

The most fun of all, however, is to look at pieces of driftwood as you find them just to see what creature, animal or object the natural shape may resemble. The search itself can be as rewarding as what you make or do with your finds.

make outdoor furniture for your doll's tea party

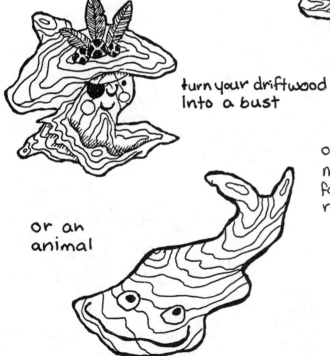
turn your driftwood into a bust

or an animal

or varnish to make a sculpture for your room

WATERSHIP UP

No matter what kind of waterway is close by — creek, lake, stream or even a mud puddle — you can make boats to float or sail from natural materials. Try constructing some of these, and then make up some of your own.

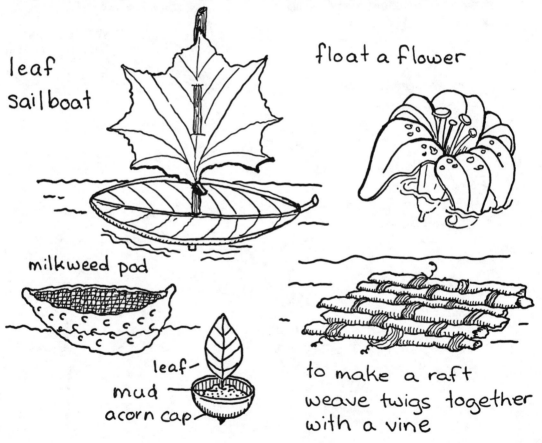

leaf
sailboat

float a flower

milkweed pod

leaf-
mud
acorn cap

to make a raft
weave twigs together
with a vine

73

QUICKIES
Just For Fun With Treasures From The Water's Edge

As you walk along the creek, river or lake's edge, look for watercress for a salad or mint for tea. You won't find them everywhere, but searching can be so much fun.

Collect small stones that have been washed and smoothed by the water to use for game markers or good-luck charms. Some people think carrying a round white stone brings good luck. Search until you find one that feels just right in your pocket.

Find one lovely shell with a hole in it to hang on a string and wear around your neck.

Collect tiny plants to make a mini dish garden for your windowsill.

Make sand angels.

PACK IT UP AND SHIP IT OUT

One of the nicest things you can do for someone special, is to share some of the wonderful and unusual things you find on your nature hunts. As you become more accustomed to looking for nature's treasures, you will often see just the right thing to send for a special holiday or birthday greeting, to someone who's sick or just as a message to brighten someone's day.

One of the wonderful things about nature is that many plants live and grow in only one type of environment and are found no where else. Each part of the country has its own storehouse of nature's surprises.

Therefore, it is especially fun to send something from your own area to someone in another town or state. You might even develop a "pen pal" you have never seen to "swap" treasures with. While sending and receiving some very "natural" mail, you would also be learning more about the world of nature beyond your own turf. One good way to do this would be to ask a family friend or relative in a faraway place to help you exchange addresses with a girl or boy just about your age who likes to explore and enjoy nature as much as you do.

76

To send natural materials in envelopes, you need to enclose the objects in some soft paper (bathroom or facial tissue is good and paper towels or napkins will work, but not quite as well). Then, wrap that package in a piece of tissue paper or aluminum foil and tape it together. Some things that can be shipped safely in envelopes include pressed ferns, leaves or flowers; feathers, mosses, lichens and dried herbs.

Seedpods, shells, rocks, bark and small pieces of driftwood will need to be wrapped carefully and shipped in boxes. You probably would want to save these for special times or just collect them to give to people you can "hand deliver" them to.

Palmetto leaves

Spanish moss

pine cone

cotton bolls

INDEX